THE RECKONING

TRUTH, JUSTICE, AND HEALING

A Truth and Reconciliation Commission to Heal a Betrayed Nation

MARY KNAPP

THE RECKONING
TRUTH, JUSTICE, AND HEALING
A TRUTH and RECONCILIATION COMMISSION to HEAL a
BETRAYED NATION

Dedication

To my Beloved Children:

You are the song of love my soul never stops singing.
I offer these pages as prayer.
Because of you, I abide always in faith and hope.
Because of you, I dream of a brighter world.
Because of you, I strive for a future where you
—and all children—
can live unbroken, unafraid, and unbound.

Table of Contents

Preface

Living Through the Lies

I never set out to write this book.
I set out to survive it.

To survive the madness that came when the world I trusted began to crumble — not from war or famine, but from deception. Lies were everywhere. They seeped into the news, into medicine, into the words of leaders and the silence of friends. They invaded conversations, homes, schools, churches, and even the air between us. And I watched, in real time, as truth became dangerous — as people I loved stopped recognizing one another, and the world grew more divided, more afraid, and more sick.

I saw families torn apart by propaganda.
I saw communities betray their own values to stay comfortable in the lie.
I saw fear become policy, censorship become safety, and compliance become virtue.

And I saw what it did to our souls.

The pain wasn't just political — it was personal. It crept into every corner of life. It showed up in my body, my relationships, my sleep, my sense of belonging. The world's betrayal wasn't something happening "out there." It was something I could feel — inside my own nervous system. The corruption of truth is not abstract; it's biological. It makes you sick. It eats away at hope, at trust, at joy.

That's what finally broke me open.
Not the lies themselves — but the realization that waiting for someone else to fix it was just another illusion.

I realized that truth wasn't coming to rescue us.
We were going to have to rescue truth.

The Reckoning was born from that place — from heartbreak, outrage, and a fierce, holy determination to heal what deception has shattered. Not just in the world, but in us. I wrote it as a citizen, a mother, a neighbor, a witness — someone who refuses to accept that the price of belonging is silence.

Because what happens when entire nations are built on unspoken trauma?
When the collective nervous system is hijacked by fear?
When justice becomes theater and healing becomes taboo?

We lose ourselves.
We forget that we are the keepers of truth, not the victims of those who distort it.
We forget that institutions don't have souls — people do.

So this book is my act of remembering.
It is my way of saying, *enough.*
Enough denial. Enough gaslighting. Enough pretending that we are powerless to stop what is breaking us.

It's time to face what's been done — to our minds, our families, our communities, our nation.
It's time for truth-telling to become a civic duty again.

It's time for reconciliation — not the kind that asks us to forget, but the kind that demands we *finally see.*

Because healing is not weakness.
It's the most radical form of strength there is.

This is not just a book — it's a mirror.
It asks each of us to look unflinchingly at what we've lived through, what we've believed, what we've ignored, and what we've lost.
It calls for a new kind of reckoning — not one fueled by vengeance, but by courage, clarity, and compassion.

I believe a Truth and Reconciliation process — not just at a national level, but within our communities, our families, and our own hearts — is the only path forward. Without it, we will keep repeating cycles of betrayal, denial, and decay. With it, we can begin to heal the collective wound of deception that has haunted this generation.

So here I stand — weary, but awake.
Wounded, but unwilling to look away.
Determined to speak what I know to be true:
that truth still lives,
that justice is still possible,
and that healing begins the moment we stop pretending everything is fine.

This is my reckoning.
And I hope, in some way, it becomes yours too.

— *Mary Knapp*

Introduction

The Reckoning Begins

There comes a time when the lies become unbearable. When the weight of corruption, deceit, and manipulation crushes so heavily on the human spirit that silence itself becomes complicity. That time is now.

For too long, humanity has endured the slow suffocation of systems designed not to serve us, but to exploit us. Politicians swore oaths to protect the people yet sold us to the highest bidder. Corporations poisoned our food, water, and soil while marketing death as "progress." Media empires fed us narratives crafted not to inform but to control. Big Pharma promised health while engineering dependence. Big Tech promised connection while harvesting our minds and rewriting our reality. The list of betrayals is endless.

The result? A world built on manufactured despair. A society where truth is buried under propaganda. Where justice is bought and sold. Where healing is impossible because the wounds are never allowed to close—they are kept open, festering, so the powerful can profit from our pain.

But let us be clear: this is not weakness on our part. This is not because humanity is broken. It is because **we have been enslaved by design.** Our suffering was engineered, cultivated, and enforced by those who fear what a free, conscious, awakened people might do.

And now the illusion is cracking.

The Reckoning: Truth, Justice, and Healing is written for this exact moment. It is not a polite suggestion or a distant dream. It is a demand. A declaration. A call to remember who we are and what we deserve.

The Reckoning begins with three pillars:

- **Truth**: Because without truth, there is no foundation. Lies must be exposed. Deception must be ripped out by the roots. We must name what has been done to us without hesitation or apology.
- **Justice**: Because crimes—whether committed by governments, corporations, media, or cultural elites—cannot go unanswered. Accountability is not revenge. It is the only way to ensure that corruption does not recycle itself into new disguises.
- **Healing**: Because rage and grief, as righteous as they are, must be transformed into renewal. Healing is not weakness. It is the fiercest act of resistance. To heal is to reclaim our wholeness, to refuse to remain defined by the wounds inflicted upon us.

This book will trace the layers of betrayal—political, economic, technological, psychological, emotional, and spiritual—because we must face them all. It will also outline a path forward: a Truth and Reconciliation Commission, built not as a symbolic gesture but as a living structure for accountability, restoration, and the eradication of evil from the roots.

This will not be easy work. It will demand courage, discipline, and unity. But make no mistake: the alternative is submission to permanent slavery—economic, digital, psychological, and spiritual.

We have been patient. We have endured. We have hoped that "someone else" would save us. That time is over. **The Reckoning is ours to claim.**

Let the liars and deceivers tremble. Let the profiteers and manipulators squirm. Let the architects of suffering know: their time is up.

The Reckoning has begun.

Chapter 1

The Machinery of Deception

The story of our enslavement is not one of accident. It is one of design. A vast machinery—political, psychological, economic, technological, and spiritual— has been constructed to bend human beings into submission while convincing us that we are free.

This machinery does not run on oil or steel alone. It runs on lies: lies carefully manufactured, distributed, and reinforced until they become the air we breathe. And like poisoned air, they slowly kill us from within.

To dismantle this machinery, we must see it clearly. We must call it by its true names.

Deep State and Shadow Governance
Behind the façade of elections, parties, and smiling politicians lies a darker power structure. Call it the Deep State, the Permanent Bureaucracy, or Shadow Governance—it's the hidden hand shaping policy.

These are not servants of the people. These are the guardians of empire. Unelected, unaccountable, and operating in secrecy, they control the levers of surveillance, war, finance, and law enforcement. Presidents have come and gone. Congress rises and falls. But the machinery grinds on.

Its creed is not democracy. Its creed is control.

The Deep State thrives on crisis—wars abroad, emergencies at home, endless "threats" that justify endless power. Its agents embed themselves in intelligence agencies, corporate boardrooms, think tanks, and global institutions. They decide who eats and who starves, who prospers and who is crushed. They decide what truths may be spoken, and which must be buried.

And all the while, the people are told they are free.

Psyops, Propaganda, and Media Manipulation

The most dangerous weapon in the arsenal of the Deep State is not the drone or the missile. It is the story.

Psychological operations—psyops—are crafted not for soldiers on battlefields but for civilians in their living rooms. Propaganda is no longer crude posters; it is the subtle manipulation of perception. It is the drip of false narratives, repeated until they calcify into "reality."

Media is the machine that distributes these narratives. Owned by a handful of conglomerates and beholden to the same corporate and political interests, it does not inform—it programs. It frames what you should fear, what you should desire, who you should hate, and what you must never question.

News anchors smile as they deliver scripts written by unseen hands. Entertainment saturates with hidden messages. Social platforms pretend to connect us while curating thought and silencing dissent. Algorithms decide what you see, what you know, and eventually, what you believe.

This is not journalism. It is mind control dressed as information.

The Cost of Deception

The machinery of deception does not simply distort reality—it manufactures it. It tells us enemies exist where none do, and hides enemies where they operate freely. It convinces us that endless war is peace, that toxic food is nourishment, that slavery is freedom.

The cost of living under such manipulation is not only economic or political. It is psychological. It is spiritual. It fractures our ability to trust—not just systems, but each other. It pits neighbor against neighbor, citizen against citizen, until we are too divided to unite against the true architects of our suffering.

And that is precisely the point. A divided people are an easily ruled people.

Breaking the Spell

To face this truth is painful. It demands we admit we have been deceived, controlled, and enslaved. It demands we release the comforting illusion that "they" have our best interests at heart. But only in facing this pain can we be free.

The first act of resistance is seeing. Naming the lie. Refusing the narrative. Shattering the illusion.

Once the spell is broken, the machinery cannot run. It requires our consent—our belief in its stories, our participation in its games. Withdraw that consent, and its gears begin to grind to a halt.

The Reckoning begins here—with eyes wide open, with the courage to see the machinery for what it is, and with a vow: never again will humanity allow itself to be chained by lies.

Reflection & Journaling Prompts

Facing the Hidden Hand
- Where in your own life have you felt the presence of hidden power shaping outcomes beyond your control?
- How does naming the "Deep State" or "Shadow Governance" shift your perception of politics and authority?

Unmasking the Narrative
- Recall a time when you discovered that something you believed (from media, school, or government) was a lie.
- What emotions surfaced when you realized the truth—rage, grief, betrayal, liberation?

Breaking the Spell
- What propaganda or narrative do you now refuse to accept, even if those around you still believe it?
- Where do you see the machinery of deception trying to divide you from others in your community, family, or nation?

Reclaiming Power
- If propaganda thrives on consent, how can you begin withdrawing your consent in daily life?
- What practical steps can you take to reclaim your own mind, and to share truth with others?

The Vow of Awareness
- Write a personal vow that declares your refusal to be enslaved by lies again.
- What commitments will you make to protect yourself—and humanity—against future deception?

Chapter 2

Institutional Betrayals

If the machinery of deception is the system's mind, then institutional betrayal is its body. It is the hands that carry out orders, the legs that march us into submission, the mouth that smiles as it twists the knife deeper.

Institutions were meant to serve humanity. Instead, they were weaponized against us. They became predators, and we—citizens, patients, workers, voters—were reduced to prey.

The rage we feel is not misplaced. It is righteous. Because these betrayals did not happen only in the shadows. They happened in broad daylight—behind podiums, in courtrooms, in hospital wards, on TV screens. Always cloaked in authority. Always demanding our trust.

It is time to strip away the cloak.

Health Care and Big Pharma: Profit Over People

Health is sacred. It is the foundation of life itself. Yet health care was sold to the highest bidder. Instead of healing the sick, the system became an industry of exploitation.

Pharmaceutical giants engineered a business model not of curing, but of managing disease. They turned human suffering into recurring revenue—pills for profit, treatments for dependency, lifelong patients instead of thriving people.

Doctors became sales reps. Hospitals became billing centers. Regulators became revolving-door employees of the very corporations they were supposed to oversee. And the people? Reduced to test subjects, walking profit centers, resources drained for dividends.

They promised health. They delivered dependence—and sometimes injury, illness, and death.

Judicial Failures and Systemic Corruption

Justice was meant to be blind. Instead, she is bought.

The courts—judges, prosecutors, institutions of law—have been corrupted to protect power rather than uphold it. Ordinary citizens face the full weight of punishment, while elites walk free no matter their crimes. Wealth buys immunity. Influence buys silence. Connections buy escape.

The system prosecutes the poor, shields the powerful, and grinds ordinary people into dust. Victims are retraumatized, whistleblowers silenced, truth-seekers punished. Courtrooms become theaters where outcomes are scripted long before proceedings begin.

This is not justice. It is performance for the masses while corruption festers behind the curtain.

Political Actors and the Erosion of Trust

Elected officials—those sworn to represent us—sold us out. Again and again, they promised reform while cashing checks from lobbyists. Their allegiance was not to the people, but to the donors who financed their campaigns.

Public trust is the lifeblood of democracy. And it has been drained dry. Politicians no longer even pretend to listen—they perform. They smile, wave, and posture for cameras while quietly signing deals that strip us of rights, freedom, and wealth.

Representation has become performance art, staged by actors reading scripts written by corporate sponsors. The betrayal is not subtle. It is systemic.

Rigged Elections and the Theft of a Right

The vote is sacred. It is the voice of the people, the cornerstone of democracy. But that voice has been tampered with, suppressed, and silenced.

Gerrymandering redraws districts to predetermine outcomes. Electronic machines are riddled with vulnerabilities. Mail-in systems are exploited. Ballots vanish. Tallies are manipulated.

And when citizens demand answers, they are mocked as "conspiracy theorists," silenced by the very institutions sworn to protect their right to be heard.

What is left of democracy when the ballot is a lie? What remains of freedom when the people's will is filtered through a rigged machine?

Media Propaganda and Lies

The media was supposed to hold power accountable. Instead, it became the propaganda arm of the very forces it was meant to expose.

Night after night, talking heads tell us what to think, what to fear, who to blame. They decide which stories matter and which truths must never be spoken. Lies are repeated until accepted as fact. Truth is buried beneath layers of distraction, spin, and manufactured outrage.

They are not watchdogs. They are gatekeepers. Not truth-tellers, but storytellers in service of empire.

And the cost? A fractured society—divided by false narratives, blinded by outrage, unable to see the real architects of our suffering.

The Reckoning With Betrayal

To face institutional betrayal is to confront grief, rage, and despair. But in that fire lies the possibility of rebirth. For once we see that our institutions are not merely broken—but deliberately corrupted—we can stop clinging to illusions and start demanding transformation.

We must tear down what has been weaponized against us and build anew, rooted in truth, justice, and healing.

Anything less is submission.

The Reckoning will not allow submission.

Reflection & Journaling Prompts

The Betrayal of Health
- How have you or someone you love been harmed by a health care system that put profit before healing?
- What emotions surface when you reflect on this exploitation?

When Justice Failed
- Have you ever witnessed or experienced corruption in the judicial system?
- How did it affect your trust in the idea of "justice"?

Losing Faith in Politics
- What moment first shattered your trust in political leaders or the electoral process?
- How does it feel to admit that betrayal openly?

Media Lies
- Recall a lie from the media that shaped public perception—and later proved false.
- How has this shifted your relationship to news and information sources?

A Vow Against Betrayal
- Write a personal vow declaring that you will no longer allow corrupted institutions to define truth, justice, or health for you.
- What steps can you take to build trust in truth outside of these failing systems?

Chapter 3

Corporations and Collusion

The betrayal of institutions would not be complete without their corporate accomplices—the predators in suits who turned human life into raw material for profit. Behind every poisoned river, every unaffordable hospital bill, every silenced voice on the internet, there is a corporation pulling strings, writing laws, and cashing checks.

These corporations do not compete so much as collude. They form cartels with governments, banks, and global councils, binding us into a web of surveillance, exploitation, and control. They are the architects of a dystopian future where human beings are reduced to data points, consumers, and slaves.

The mask of "progress" and "innovation" hides a machinery of domination. It is time to rip it away.

Big Tech: Censorship and Surveillance
They promised connection. They delivered chains.

Big Tech built platforms that became the public square, then rigged them to silence dissent. Voices that challenge official narratives are shadow-banned, demonetized, or erased altogether. Censorship is dressed as "safety," but its true purpose is obedience.

Every click, every keystroke, every movement is tracked and stored. Your life is no longer private—it is harvested, analyzed, and sold to the highest bidder. Surveillance capitalism has turned your existence into a commodity. And when governments want to monitor, manipulate, or crush opposition, they need only tap the data streams these corporations have already built.

This is not freedom. It is digital slavery.

Big Insurance: Exploiting Fear

Insurance was meant to offer protection. Instead, it became legalized extortion: pay endlessly, or risk ruin. Denials and delays are baked into the model, leaving people bankrupt at their most vulnerable.

Like parasites, insurers thrive on fear. They extract wealth while offering little security, and when disaster strikes, they vanish behind red tape and fine print. Their loyalty is not to people, but to profit margins.

We are forced to gamble with our lives, paying into a system that is designed to win.

Economic Enslavement: Bankers and the Financial System

The modern economy is not built for prosperity—it is engineered for bondage.

Central banks and global financial institutions create money as debt, lend it at interest, and enforce repayment with ruthless precision. Citizens labor for lifetimes not to create wealth, but to service obligations they never agreed to.

Credit hooks are dangled as convenience and chained as traps; wages stagnate while inflation eats away at savings. The bankers profit no matter what, tightening the screws as economies buckle.

This is not economics. It is financial warfare.

Global Collusion and the Consolidation of Power

Behind the curtain, unelected and influential bodies sketch blueprints for a future where freedom is optional. Their slogans and frameworks—marketed as inevitabilities—often read less like policy and more like architecture for control.

These entities collude with governments and corporations to centralize power, digitize currency, surveil transactions, and engineer dependence. They envision systems where human behavior is measurable, scored, and managed—leaving little room for dissent or escape.

This is not progress. It is a quiet consolidation of power.

Big Agriculture: Poisoning the Planet

The food meant to nourish us has been corrupted. Seeds are engineered for corporate profit, soils are stripped by chemicals, and animals are pumped with hormones and antibiotics. Crops are doused in poisons while marketing assures us it is "safe."

The consequences are visible in our bodies—rising rates of chronic illness, fertility issues, autoimmune conditions, and cancers. The very act of eating can become a slow form of chemical warfare.

Beyond food, the air is polluted, the water tainted with industrial runoff and pharmaceuticals, and soils collapsing under extractive practices. This is not negligence. It is assault.

The Reckoning With Collusion

Corporations, banks, insurers, and global elites collude not to serve life, but to extract it. They poison, exploit, surveil, and silence with impunity because they believe they are untouchable.

But nothing made by human hands is immune to human hands. Systems built in secrecy can be exposed in sunlight. Chains forged in boardrooms can be broken by collective resolve.

The Reckoning demands we strip the mask of legitimacy from these entities, expose their harms, and create alternatives rooted in life, not profit; truth, not deception; freedom, not control.

We are not their livestock. We are not their debt-slaves. We are not their data points. We are human beings—and we will be free.

Reflection & Journaling Prompts

The Digital Cage
- How has censorship or surveillance affected your life?
- What freedoms have you lost—or risked losing—because of Big Tech's reach?

The Economics of Chains
- Reflect on your relationship with debt, credit, or banking systems.
- How does it feel to name these systems as tools of enslavement rather than neutral "services"?

The Poisoned Earth
- Where do you feel most betrayed by the food, air, water, or soil around you?
- How has this awareness shifted your choices in what you eat, drink, or buy?

The Global Plot
- How do you respond to the idea that powerful global bodies are scripting futures that limit freedom?
- What emotions—rage, fear, defiance—does this recognition stir?

The Vow of Liberation
- Write a vow declaring you will not consent to corporate slavery, poisoning, or surveillance.
- What first steps can you take today to reclaim sovereignty over your body, mind, and resources?

Chapter 4

The Commerce of Evil

If the machinery of deception is the mind, and corrupted institutions its body, then the commerce of evil is its blood—flowing through every dark artery of the world, enriching the few by consuming the many.

This is not capitalism. This is not trade. This is predation on a planetary scale. It is the deliberate trafficking of weapons, drugs, humans, organs, and children—the most depraved commerce imaginable—profiting the same elites, bankers, corporations, and shadow actors who lecture us about morality while feasting on human misery.

At this level, the mask of legitimacy falls away. What remains is raw evil, sustained by secrecy, enforced by violence, and protected by power.

Weapons Trafficking: Wars for Profit
Every war you've seen—every "conflict," every covert operation—has a market behind it. Weapons trafficking is among the most lucrative industries on Earth, and it thrives not on peace, but on perpetual war.

Arms dealers, defense contractors, and covert agencies profit when conflict endures. They supply both sides, stoke tensions, and flood regions with tools of death. Human beings become collateral, nations become markets, and blood becomes profit.

This is not defense. It is business.

Drug Trafficking: Addiction by Design

The so-called "war on drugs" is itself a lie. Governments, intelligence agencies, and corporate actors have colluded—knowingly or through negligence—to flood communities with narcotics while profiting at every stage: production, distribution, policing, and incarceration.

From illicit drugs on foreign soil to prescription opioids in suburban pharmacies, addiction has been engineered as a mechanism of control. Families are torn apart, lives are destroyed, and entire communities are left hollow while cartels and their silent partners rake in billions.

They promised protection. They delivered an endless supply.

Human Trafficking: Flesh as Currency

Across borders and in the shadows of cities, human beings are bought and sold as if slavery never ended—because in many ways, it never did. Millions are trafficked for labor, sexual exploitation, and forced servitude, their existence erased, their suffering hidden.

This is not a crime of the powerless alone. It is sustained by networks of wealth and influence. Traffickers operate with impunity when officials look away, when protection is for sale, and when profit trumps humanity.

Slavery did not die. It evolved.

Organ Harvesting: The Darkest Market

Bodies themselves have become commodities. Organ harvesting—targeting the most vulnerable, including prisoners, refugees, and the trafficked—feeds a black market that intersects with hospitals, brokers, and global demand.

This is commerce stripped of conscience. Human beings reduced to spare parts, lives extinguished for profit. And those in power often look the other way.

The Depravity of Child Exploitation

At the heart of this nightmare is the most unspeakable crime: the trafficking, abuse, and exploitation of children. This is the ultimate corruption—innocence stolen, childhood destroyed, futures ruined beyond repair.

Powerful networks protect predators; victims are silenced, discredited, or destroyed. When the most vulnerable are preyed upon by the most powerful, a society has crossed the line into absolute moral collapse.

This is not fringe. This is a rot at the center of systems that claim to protect us.

The Reckoning With Evil

Weapons. Drugs. Slaves. Organs. Children. All traded, trafficked, and consumed for the profit and pleasure of the few. This is not merely corruption. It is depravity—the inversion of every human value.

To acknowledge this is to stand at the gates of grief and rage. It is to confront the abyss. But in that confrontation lies unshakable resolve: such evil must be uprooted—not managed, not normalized, not negotiated with—but eradicated at its source.

The Reckoning demands exposure and accountability. Every trafficker, every profiteer, every enabler—no matter how protected—must be named, investigated, and held to justice. For the living. For the memory of the lost. For the children who deserve a world without monsters.

There can be no healing without this cleansing fire.

Reflection & Journaling Prompts

Confronting the Abyss
- How does it feel to accept that slavery, trafficking, and child exploitation are present in the world today?
- What emotions rise in you—rage, grief, disbelief, resolve?

The Cost of Silence
- Where have you seen silence protect predators—at work, in institutions, or in your community?
- How has that silence shaped outcomes for victims?

The Sacred Duty
- What does protecting children mean to you on the deepest level?
- How does that conviction inform the future you are willing to fight for?

Naming the Enemy

- Which aspect of this commerce of evil feels most urgent to confront for you—weapons, drugs, human slavery, organ trafficking, or child exploitation? Why?

The Vow of Eradication

- Write a vow that such evil will never be tolerated on this planet again.
- What concrete first steps—however small—can you take today to embody that vow?

Chapter 5

Psychological and Spiritual Warfare

If weapons and poisons destroy bodies, and corruption devours nations, then psychological and spiritual warfare strikes at the very essence of humanity.

This is the war most people never see, though it shapes every thought, every feeling, every belief we hold. It is the silent battlefield where trauma is manufactured, values are inverted, faith is mocked, and despair is engineered as policy.

The enemy has always known: if you can break the spirit, you can enslave the body without resistance. And so they came for our minds, our emotions, our very souls.

Trauma Programming: Breaking the Human Spirit
From childhood to adulthood, trauma is not accidental—it is manufactured. War, abuse, poverty, indoctrination, and media saturation are not random misfortunes. They are deliberate assaults designed to keep humanity fractured and docile.

Traumatized people are easier to control. Fearful people obey. Shattered families create isolated individuals who are too busy surviving to resist. Trauma becomes the invisible prison around our collective psyche.

We were conditioned to expect pain, to normalize abuse, to accept despair as natural. And every time we tried to rise, they broke us again.

Inversion of Values: Good Made Evil, Evil Made Good

They mocked truth as conspiracy. They exalted lies as fact. They painted predators as philanthropists and branded whistleblowers as criminals.

They glorified greed and called it success. They trivialized compassion and called it weakness. They sexualized children and called it liberation. They inverted the sacred into the profane, and the profane into the sacred.

This was no random moral drift. It was a calculated inversion—the deliberate confusion of human values, so people no longer knew what was real, what was good, what was worth defending.

When values are inverted, humanity stumbles in darkness. And in darkness, predators rule.

The Destruction of Faith

Faith has always been humanity's shield—faith in God, in truth, in each other, in the unseen current of good that runs through the cosmos. That shield had to be broken.

Religion was twisted into dogma and control. Spirituality was mocked as superstition. Communities of worship were infiltrated, divided, and hollowed out. Science was weaponized—not as a path to truth, but as a priesthood of obedience.

They wanted humanity to believe in nothing but the system. To trust no power higher than the state, no truth deeper than the screen, no hope beyond what corporations sold.

For if we stop believing in the sacred, we stop believing in ourselves.

Engineered Despair: A World Without Hope

Why do so many live with anxiety, depression, and despair? Why do suicides rise, families collapse, and addictions multiply?

Because despair has been engineered.

The news is designed to overwhelm. The economy is rigged to exhaust. Entertainment numbs rather than uplifts. Education produces workers, not thinkers. Technology isolates while pretending to connect.

Every day we are told the world is ending, that humanity is doomed, that we are powerless. This despair is not incidental—it is policy. A broken, hopeless population will never rise.

The Reckoning With the War for the Soul

To confront psychological and spiritual warfare is to feel both rage and grief. It is to look in the mirror and see scars you did not choose, wounds you did not deserve. It is to realize that your pain was someone else's profit, your despair someone else's plan.

But it is also to discover the ember that never went out—the ember of resistance, of faith, of love that survived every assault.

That ember is why we are still here. It is why the Reckoning is possible. For no matter how much they tried to break us, we did not shatter completely.

The Reckoning will not only expose this war. It will end it. It will reclaim truth, restore values, rekindle faith, and banish despair. Humanity will rise from trauma, not as slaves, but as survivors who refuse to bow again.

Reflection & Journaling Prompts

The Wound and the Chain
- Where in your life have you felt trauma used as a tool of control— within family, school, religion, or society?
- How has this trauma shaped the way you see yourself and others?

Inverted Values
- What values did society teach you that now feel false or inverted?
- How did believing those lies affect your choices?

The Faith That Remains
- What have you lost faith in?
- What, if anything, has your faith survived?

The Machinery of Despair
- Where do you feel despair has been engineered into your life—news, work, relationships, media?
- How do you resist it, even in small ways?

The Vow of the Soul
- Write a vow declaring that your spirit will not be broken.
- What practices or actions will you commit to, to guard and strengthen your mind, heart, and soul?

Chapter 6

Planetary Control and the Digital Prison Systems

If the earlier layers of deception and corruption were weapons of enslavement, the emerging control systems are the chains now fastened around humanity's neck.

We are not simply being poisoned, propagandized, and traumatized. We are being digitally caged — corralled into a surveillance grid so vast and intrusive that even Orwell could not have imagined it. The new prison has no bars, no walls, no guards in towers. It is built of code, satellites, algorithms, biometric scans, and centralized systems that decide who is free and who is condemned.

And its architects call it "progress."

The Rise of AI Surveillance
Every phone. Every camera. Every microphone. Every sensor.

All wired into systems that know where we go, what we buy, what we say, what we feel — even what we think.

Artificial Intelligence is not a neutral tool. It is being trained to profile, predict, and control human beings. Social credit systems, predictive policing, algorithmic censorship — all justified as "safety" or "efficiency."

But safety for whom? Efficiency for what?

The truth is brutal: surveillance is not for our protection. It is for our containment.

CBDCs and Biometric IDs: The Currency of Chains
Banking cartels and globalist institutions are rushing toward Central Bank Digital Currencies (CBDCs) — programmable money tied to biometric identity. At first it will look convenient. Then the cage door will close.

With a keystroke, access to food, travel, medicine, or housing can be denied. With an algorithm, dissent can be punished. With a digital wallet, freedom itself can be switched off.

This same system promises "inclusion" while ensuring total exclusion for anyone who dares resist. This is not freedom. It is economic enslavement with an on/off switch.

Transhumanism: The Assault on Human Biology
Beyond surveillance and currency, the new order seeks to rewrite humanity itself.

Genetic manipulation. Neural implants. Synthetic biology. Merging man with machine.

All sold as "enhancement" while in truth they are experiments in ownership. A chipped, engineered, modified human is no longer fully human — they are property.

The dream of the elites is not liberation, but patenting life itself: to own your DNA, edit your children, and colonize the human body as they once colonized nations.

Climate Manipulation and Environmental Control
We are told the planet is dying and only global control can save it. But the same powers poisoning the air, water, soil, and food now preach about "sustainability."

Behind the curtain lies geoengineering, weather manipulation, and manufactured scarcity. They weaponize the climate while posing as its saviors. They burn the Earth, then sell us the ashes as progress.

The climate agenda is not about protecting nature. It is about controlling humanity through fear, restriction, and rationing.

The Digital Prison
Imagine a world where:
* Your speech is censored by algorithms.

- Your money is programmed by governments.
- Your body is monitored by biometric scanners.
- Your thoughts are nudged by AI.
- Your movements are tracked, recorded, and scored.

This is not a nightmare of tomorrow. It is being built now — piece by piece, app by app, policy by policy, crisis by crisis.

And once complete, it will be the perfect prison: invisible, inescapable, and justified in the name of "the common good."

The Reckoning With Control

We must face the truth: they are building a planetary system of slavery and calling it freedom. The technology of convenience is the machinery of control.

But technology is not destiny. Control is not inevitable. Humanity still has the choice to resist, to reject, to rebuild.

The Reckoning demands that we see this digital prison for what it is — not a future threat, but a present reality. Only then can we tear it down and replace it with systems rooted in transparency, accountability, and human dignity.

Reflection & Journaling Prompts

The Cage You Feel
- Where in your daily life do you already feel the weight of digital surveillance or control?
- How does it affect the way you speak, move, or interact?

The Currency of Chains
- What would it mean if your access to money or resources could be shut off by policy or algorithm?
- How do you imagine resisting that control?

The Assault on Humanity
- How do you feel about the push toward merging humans with machines?

- Where do you draw the line between technology as tool and technology as prison?

The Fear Narrative
- What fear-based narratives (climate, disease, security) do you now recognize as pretexts for control?
- How do you reframe these narratives in your own life without giving in to despair?

The Vow of Freedom
- Write a vow declaring that you will not consent to digital slavery.
- What actions, however small, can you take to defend your autonomy in a digitized world?

Chapter 7

The Human Cost

All the machinery of deception, corruption, trafficking, and digital enslavement points to one undeniable outcome: human suffering. This is not theory, not abstract policy, not some distant conspiracy. It is visible everywhere — in hollowed-out faces, in grief carved into families, in the empty places where trust and hope once lived.

We must name this cost. We must not look away. For behind every statistic is a human soul — wounded, abandoned, or destroyed by systems built for profit and power.

The Epidemic of Mental Collapse

Anxiety. Depression. Addiction. Suicide.

No longer rare, no longer shocking. They have become the baseline. Entire generations medicated into numbness. Children raised on screens, unable to focus or connect. Elders abandoned to despair and loneliness.

This is not the byproduct of a busy world. It is the result of engineered despair. People are breaking under the weight of lies, isolation, and pressure to conform.

And instead of healing the wound, the system monetizes it. Broken minds mean profits for Big Pharma. Profits for prisons. Profits for propaganda.

Broken Communities

Where once there was neighborhood and kinship, now there is surveillance and suspicion. Where once we gathered to celebrate, mourn, or share, now we scroll in isolation.

Communities have been atomized — families divided by politics, friends split by propaganda, generations alienated from one another. The natural fabric of human life — connection, belonging, support — has been deliberately shredded.

A fractured population cannot rise together. That was always the plan.

Economic Devastation

The middle class gutted. Small businesses destroyed. Workers exploited, then discarded. Entire populations reduced to debt slaves.

While the few gorge themselves on trillions, the many work longer hours for less security, crushed under interest rates, inflation, and manufactured scarcity. Parents fear for their children's futures. Children inherit a world where housing, education, and stability feel like impossible dreams.

This devastation is not a natural cycle. It is engineered theft. Plunder on a planetary scale.

Loss of Trust, Hope, and Sovereignty

What does it mean to live in a world where you no longer trust your leaders, your media, your doctors, your elections — even your neighbors?

It means disorientation. Doubting your own instincts. Surrendering to whatever narrative seems safest in the moment, even if it is a lie.

This destruction of trust is perhaps the deepest wound. For without trust, hope dies. Without hope, sovereignty evaporates. Without sovereignty, humanity becomes a herd waiting for slaughter.

The Loneliness of Division

Propaganda divides families. Elections split households. Social media drives wedges between friends. Lovers break under the strain of conflicting narratives.

The cost is counted in empty chairs at dinner tables, estranged siblings, broken marriages, friendships turned bitter. It is counted in children who no longer know who to trust, because the very people they love are at war with one another.

This is the human battlefield — not in distant lands, but in our living rooms, schools, and kitchens.

The Reckoning With Suffering

We must face the human cost with open eyes and broken hearts. Only then do we grasp the true magnitude of the crimes committed against us.

The suffering was not an accident. Not an unintended consequence. It was the point. A divided, broken, hopeless humanity is easy to govern, easy to exploit, easy to silence.

But if they believed suffering would destroy us completely, they miscalculated. For every broken heart still beats. For every fractured community, a hunger for connection burns. For every soul pushed to despair, another is ready to rise.

The Reckoning begins with grief, but it does not end there. The cost has been unbearable — and it will be the proof of why this system must never be allowed to rise again.

Reflection & Journaling Prompts

The Wounds You Carry
- How has this era of lies and division personally impacted your mental health, your hope, or your trust?
- Where do you feel the deepest wounds?

Loss and Division
- Who have you lost — in relationships, community, or trust — because of propaganda or systemic corruption?
- How do you honor that loss without letting it destroy you?

The Cost You Witness
- Where do you see the suffering most clearly in your community?
- How does it fuel your desire for truth and justice?

The Hunger for Connection
- Despite division, where do you still see sparks of unity, compassion, or shared humanity?
- How can you nurture those sparks in your own life?

The Vow of the Heart
- Write a vow declaring that the suffering you have endured or witnessed will not be wasted.
- How will you transform grief into fuel for healing and resistance?

Chapter 8

The Right to Truth

The Reckoning turns here. After rage and grief, after the unveiling of corruption and control, we stand at the threshold of the one thing that can heal and restore: Truth.

Truth is not optional. It is not a luxury. It is not a privilege to be granted when convenient. Truth is a right — intrinsic, unalienable, rooted in biology, psychology, morality, survival, and in the very nature of God and creation.

When truth is denied, people fracture. Families collapse. Societies disintegrate. Nations rot from within.

When truth is honored, people thrive. Communities flourish. Justice becomes possible. Hope returns.

Truth is not merely information. It is the foundation of human dignity, freedom, and life itself.

Social Cohesion and Cooperation

Humans are social beings. We depend on one another to survive. Communities cannot function without trust, and trust cannot exist without truth.

Lies corrode relationships, sow division, and breed violence. Truth binds us in a shared reality.

From hunting and gathering to building civilizations, survival has always depended on honesty. A society that abandons truth collapses into suspicion and betrayal.

Evolutionary and Survival Factors

Evolution favored those who could see reality clearly. Tribes that lied about predators, weather, or resources did not survive. Truth is not abstract philosophy. It is biology. It is survival.

To distort or suppress truth is to place humanity back in mortal danger. To live in lies is to break the most basic law of life: perceive reality — or perish.

Moral and Ethical Values

Every culture, every religion, every moral code has upheld truth as sacred. To deceive, to manipulate, to bear false witness — always condemned.

Truth is the foundation of justice. Without it, the innocent are punished, the guilty walk free, and the vulnerable are preyed upon.

To deny truth is to deny morality itself.

Psychological Well-Being

The human psyche craves truth the way the body craves air. Lies suffocate the mind. They produce confusion, despair, anxiety, and depression.

Trauma survivors know this: healing begins with truth. You cannot heal what you cannot name. Denial and secrecy perpetuate the wound. Truth-telling opens the path to restoration.

Equality and Social Mobility

Without truth, equality is impossible. Lies shield the powerful and crush the powerless. Corruption thrives on secrecy.

Truth levels the field. It exposes the hidden deals and false narratives. It gives the poor, the oppressed, the marginalized the chance to rise.

Truth is the oxygen of justice.

Restoration of Balance

Lies destabilize the world. Justice falters. Economies collapse. Communities divide. Nature itself is plundered.

Truth restores equilibrium. Every reckoning in history — the fall of tyrants, the end of slavery, civil rights struggles, reconciliation movements — began with truth-telling.

Truth is always the first step toward balance and renewal.

Universal Human Rights

International law already recognizes truth as a right in the aftermath of war crimes, crimes against humanity, and systemic abuses. Survivors have the right to know what was done, who did it, and how justice will be secured.

The right to truth is not theoretical. It is enshrined in the conscience of humanity.

The American Predicate: God-Given Rights

The U.S. Declaration of Independence rests on a foundation that cannot be ignored:

- There exists a Creator.
- From that Creator, all humans are made equal.
- From equality, humans are endowed with unalienable rights — life, liberty, and the pursuit of happiness.
- Governments exist to secure those rights.
- When governments destroy them, the people have the authority to alter or abolish them.

This predicate is clear: rights do not come from governments, kings, corporations, or elites. They flow from a higher source.

The right to Truth follows directly. For without truth, life is endangered, liberty denied, happiness destroyed. To lie to the people is to strip them of their God-given rights.

Truth as a Sacred and Inalienable Right

Human biology craves it.
Human psychology needs it.
Human morality demands it.
Human survival depends on it.
God ordains it.

Truth is as essential as food, water, and air. To deny it is to starve the soul. To suppress it is to commit spiritual murder.

And so we declare: **Truth is an unalienable human right.**

No government, no corporation, no media empire, no cartel, no "Deep State" has the authority to strip humanity of this right. To live in truth is not a request. It is a birthright.

Reflection & Journaling Prompts

Your Hunger for Truth
- Where in your life do you feel the deepest hunger for truth?
- What lies have caused you the most suffering?

Truth and Trust
- How has the absence of truth eroded your trust in leaders, institutions, or relationships?
- What would restored truth make possible?

Truth as Survival
- When have you experienced truth as life-saving, healing, or liberating?
- What truths do you refuse to betray, no matter the cost?

Your Constitutional Birthright
- Reflect on the idea of God-given, unalienable rights.
- How does the right to truth flow naturally from life, liberty, and the pursuit of happiness?

The Vow of Truth
- Write a vow declaring your commitment to seek, speak, and defend truth — for yourself, your community, and the generations to come.

Chapter 9

A Truth and Reconciliation Commission, The Path Forward

The lies and corruption are unraveling. And as they do, a monstrous backlash is coming — a tidal wave of rage, grief, and shock that will rock our nation and our world to the core. When the truth bursts into daylight, trust in public figures, institutions, and systems — local, state, national, and international — will rupture on a scale we have never seen before.

We cannot pretend this reckoning will be orderly. We cannot assume people will simply "move on." The betrayals have been too deep. The damage too severe. The wounds too personal. Our nation already trembles under collective trauma, and the eruption of full truth will unleash a storm of PTSD on both an individual and societal scale.

That is why we must prepare. That is why we need more than outrage, more than scattered justice, more than vengeance. We need a national structure, a mechanism, a container to guide and transform the inescapable process of reckoning. Without it, chaos will consume us. With it, we have a chance — not only to survive this eruption, but to transmute it into truth, accountability, and healing.

That structure is a Truth and Reconciliation Commission.

Justice: The Role of Courts and Prosecutions

Of course, there must be legal redress. Crimes must be prosecuted. Perpetrators — at every level, from global actors to national leaders, state officials, and local collaborators — must face the full weight of the law. Retributive justice is necessary. The people must see that accountability is real, that perpetrators are not untouchable, that no office, no uniform, no title shields anyone from consequences.

But here is the hard reality: not every offender will stand trial. Evidence will be missing. Cases will collapse. Loopholes will be exploited. The courts, as vital as they are, cannot carry the full weight of this reckoning. Too many will escape the reach of the gavel.

Filling the Gap: The Role of a TRC

This is where a Truth and Reconciliation Commission becomes indispensable. A TRC does not replace the courts; it supplements them. It fills the gap between what can be legally proven and what is morally undeniable.

At their heart, TRCs are not only about punishment — they are about harm, accountability, and healing. They allow victims to be seen and heard. They give space for survivors to confront perpetrators, to ask the burning questions:

- Why did you participate?
- How could you contribute to such a travesty?
- Do you see the damage you have caused?
- What will you do to ensure this never happens again?

For offenders, a TRC strips away the mask of anonymity. It demands a moral inventory. It forces acknowledgment. Even when courts cannot convict, a TRC makes silence impossible and ensures history cannot be rewritten by the victors.

Why TRCs Matter: Repairing the Fabric of Humanity

The lies and corruption of the past decades have not only destroyed lives; they have shredded relationships and communities. Families torn apart by propaganda. Neighbors divided by politics. Trust demolished between citizens and institutions.

Human beings are not isolated units. We are bound in webs of relationship. To betray that bond is to wound the essence of humanity itself. A TRC creates space to repair those bonds. It does not promise instant healing — but it offers the conditions under which healing becomes possible.

By facing truth together, families can mend. Communities can rebuild. Nations can rediscover cohesion. Humanity can begin to knit itself back together after the engineered divisions of propaganda, war, and systemic corruption.

The Deeper Healing

A TRC is not only political. It is personal. It is spiritual. It is economic. It is psychological. It is communal.

The establishment of a TRC may be our best hope to heal not just systems, but souls. It can bring forth testimony that validates the suffering so many have endured in silence. It can restore dignity where lies brought shame. It can transform grief into purpose.

And ultimately, it can remind us of the truth we already know deep in our bones: humans have an intrinsic need for fairness and justice. This is not ideology. This is biology. This is survival. This is well-being. Without fairness, we fracture. Without justice, we despair. Without truth, we perish.

The TRC is not optional. It is not abstract. It is urgent. It is necessary. It is the path forward if we are to reclaim our humanity, heal our wounds, and ensure that the atrocities we have lived through can never, ever happen again.

Reflection & Journaling Prompts

Your Demand for Justice
- Where do you most feel the hunger for accountability — in government, media, corporations, or local leadership?
- How would seeing real prosecutions or hearings change your faith in justice?

The Limits of Courts
- How do you feel when you consider that some perpetrators will never face prison?
- What does that tell you about the need for a TRC?

The Power of Testimony
- If you were given a microphone at a TRC, what truth would you speak?
- What questions would you demand of those who harmed you or your community?

Repairing Relationships
- Where have lies and corruption most deeply damaged your relationships (family, friends, neighbors)?
- How might truth-telling help restore what was lost?

The Vow of Justice and Healing
- Write a vow that you will not rest until both justice and reconciliation are pursued.
- How will you personally contribute to building a culture of truth and accountability?

Chapter 10

Building a Truth and Reconciliation Commission

This chapter draws on insights from *Truth Seeking: Elements of Creating an Effective Truth Commission*, edited by Eduardo Gonzalez, Howard Varney, Clara Ramirez-Barat, Marcie Mersky, Kelen Meregali, Stephanie Morin, and Joanna Rice. It was produced in collaboration with the Amnesty Commission of the Ministry of Brazil, the Brazilian Agency of Cooperation of the Ministry of Foreign Affairs, the International Center for Transitional Justice, and the United Nations Development Program, and prepared by the International Center for Transitional Justice in 2013. This work remains a foundational guide. It not only maps the mechanics of how truth commissions succeed, but also carries a deeper call: nations willing to confront their darkest chapters can unlock pathways to justice, healing, and renewal.

What is a Truth Commission?
A Truth Commission (TRC) is an official, nonjudicial body of limited duration, established to investigate, clarify, and acknowledge the facts, causes, and consequences of past violations of human rights.

Unlike courts, which address individual cases, TRCs examine the larger picture: the systemic patterns of abuse, the historical conditions that allowed them, and the moral responsibility of those involved.

By documenting the truth, TRCs:

- Contribute to prosecutions and reparations.
- Break cultures of silence and denial.
- Recommend reforms to prevent future abuses.
- Provide a platform for victims to be acknowledged, empowered, and heard.

TRCs are most effective when they form part of a comprehensive transitional justice strategy that includes prosecutions, reparations, and institutional reforms.

Objectives of a Truth Commission

The objectives of any TRC are defined in its founding law or decree. Typically, they aim to:

- Establish the truth about disputed or denied events.
- Protect, recognize, and empower victims and survivors.
- Contribute to accountability and deter future violations.
- Encourage institutional reform and policy change.
- Promote social and political transformation through truth-telling.

Establishing a Commission

Truth Commissions are usually created by either the executive or legislative branches of government.

- **Legislative process:** Offers stronger political backing and institutional support but can be slow and vulnerable to compromises that weaken the mandate.
- **Executive decree:** Faster to implement but may lack broad political weight.

What matters most is independence, credibility, and effectiveness. Without these, no commission can succeed.

Key Characteristics of a TRC

- **Complementary to courts.** TRCs address broad historical and social patterns of abuse, while courts focus on individual accountability.
- **Serious scope.** They investigate gross human rights violations, crimes against humanity, war crimes, economic crimes, corruption, and systemic violence.
- **Historical depth.** Investigations often cover decades to expose long-standing abuses.
- **Massive evidence base.** They collect testimony, archives, data, and employ varied methods, including statistical analysis.
- **Victim-centered approach.** Survivors remain the primary source of truth and acknowledgment.

Ensuring Strength and Credibility

To avoid repeating the failures of past "official inquiries," TRCs must safeguard their integrity:

- **Selection of members:** Commissioners must have impeccable moral and professional reputations.
- **Full independence:** Protected from political interference with legal guarantees of autonomy.
- **Transparency:** Clear procedures, codes of conduct, and open communication.
- **Civil society engagement:** Ongoing dialogue with victims, communities, and social organizations.
- **Respect for human rights:** The commission must embody the values it seeks to restore.

Legitimacy and Independence

Public trust is everything. Without legitimacy, victims will not come forward.

- **Consultative design:** Civil society, victims' groups, and affected communities must help shape the process.
- **Political and operational independence:** Commissioners must answer only to the law and the mandate, not to political interests.

Conditions for independence include:
- Transparent commissioner appointments.
- Legal safeguards against arbitrary removal.
- Protection from threats or retaliation.
- Financial, administrative, and operational autonomy.

Selecting Commissioners

Commissioners should be chosen through a transparent, consultative process involving diverse voices, especially victims.

Key considerations:
- **Size:** Usually 3–17 members, with an odd number for voting.
- **Representation:** Diversity across geography, class, religion, ethnicity, language, and gender.
- **Human rights record:** Clean history, free of corruption or abuse.
- **Neutrality:** No ties to groups under investigation.
- **Commitment:** Full-time dedication to the commission's work.
- **Expertise:** A wide range of skills — law, history, economics, anthropology, psychology, medicine, forensics, journalism, religion, and conflict resolution.

Mandate, Functions, and Powers

Objectives
- Establish facts and context.
- Restore rights and dignity to victims.
- Promote social and political reform.

Functions
- Prepare an impartial historical record.
- Gather information through documents, interviews, and testimony.
- Protect and support victims.
- Conduct outreach and education.
- Recommend policy reforms.

- Provide evidence to strengthen judicial processes.
- Promote reconciliation through truth-telling and acknowledgment.

Competence

The mandate defines:
- Types of violations under investigation.
- Time periods covered.
- Geographic scope.
- Parties involved.

Investigatory Powers

- Authority to compel testimony and documents.
- Power to request judicial orders for searches and seizures.
- Right to conduct forensic investigations, including exhumations.
- Obligation of government officials to cooperate.
- Capacity to hold public hearings with protections for vulnerable witnesses.

Procedural Rights

- Right to be heard.
- Right to legal representation.
- Right against self-incrimination.
- Witness protection programs.
- Penalties for obstruction or falsified testimony.
- Protections for commissioners acting in good faith.

Operations and Outreach

Financial Autonomy

TRCs must control their budgets while maintaining strict transparency.

Public Awareness

A communications strategy ensures that people understand the mandate, process, and opportunities to participate.

Mapping and Research
Early research helps identify the scale, patterns, and context of violations.

Regular Operations
- Collecting statements from victims and witnesses.
- Holding public hearings.
- Taking expert testimony.
- Organizing national dialogues and education campaigns.
- Providing victim support services.

Outreach and Communication
Engagement with communities ensures inclusiveness, transparency, and trust.

The Final Report and Dissolution

The TRC's work culminates in a Final Report — an official record of findings, conclusions, and recommendations.
- Reports must be widely accessible: print, online, media, archives, and libraries.
- Delivered to the head of state and relevant institutions.
- Recommendations should guide reparations, prosecutions, and reforms.
- Reports serve as permanent historical references for policymakers, educators, and future generations.

Once complete, the TRC dissolves — but its legacy lives on through the reforms, memory, and healing it has set in motion.

In short: A Truth Commission is more than an investigative body. It is a bridge between past abuses and future integrity. Designed with independence, legitimacy, and a victim-centered approach, it has the power to transform trauma into truth, silence into acknowledgment, and despair into the first steps of reconciliation.

Chapter 11

It's Time for the Truth

An Open Letter to the President...

Dear President Trump,
It is time.

On November 4, 2024, you presented the American people with a 12-point plan to dismantle the Deep State and return power to the citizens of this nation. Within that plan, one point stands above the rest in urgency and importance: your vow to establish a Truth and Reconciliation Commission to expose the hoaxes, declassify the secrets, and shine sunlight on the corruption that has poisoned our Republic.

Mr. President, the urgency of this promise cannot be overstated.

The lies and corruption of recent decades are unraveling before our eyes. These are not abstract scandals—they are open wounds in our people. The unraveling will not be neat, polite, or controlled. It will come like a tidal wave, bringing rage, grief, despair, and a rupture of trust so deep it threatens the foundation of our Republic. Families are fractured. Communities are broken. Churches hollowed. Hope extinguished. We now live in a nation where neighbors eye each other with suspicion, where friendships dissolve over propaganda, where our youth are disillusioned and our elders heartbroken.

What is coming is a reckoning. And unless there is a structure to guide it, our nation risks descending into chaos.

Prosecutions are necessary, and justice must be served in the courts of law. Perpetrators must face the weight of accountability. But not every offender will stand trial. Not every crime will leave evidence sufficient for conviction. Not every betrayal fits neatly within the frame of a courtroom. Should those victims remain unheard, their suffering unseen, their wounds untreated?

The answer is no. Absolutely not.

That is why a Truth and Reconciliation Commission is indispensable. It is the forum where the voiceless can speak, the wounded can be heard, and those who contributed to betrayal—directly or indirectly—can confront not just the law, but their conscience. It will be a national platform for truth-telling, accountability, and moral repair.

This is not only about our past—it is about our survival as a nation.

Human beings are wired—biologically, psychologically, spiritually—for truth, fairness, and justice. Deny these, and we wither. Grant them, and we rise. Without truth, there can be no trust. Without trust, no unity. And without unity, America cannot stand.

You, Mr. President, are uniquely positioned to mandate A Truth and Reconciliation Commission. The political class will not do it. The bureaucrats will not do it. The entrenched interests of the Deep State will resist it. But you have already declared your intent. You have given your word. And the people are waiting.

Issue the Executive Mandate. Establish the United States Truth and Reconciliation Commission. Give citizens the structure they need to channel their rage, grief, and broken trust into something constructive, healing, and transformative.

This is the moment to rise not only as President, but as statesman. To carve your name not merely in political history, but in the moral history of mankind.

Nations remember leaders who build monuments or win wars, but they revere those who tell the truth, restore justice, and heal their people.

Mr. President, America is bleeding. It will take nothing less than the full power of truth to stop the hemorrhage.

The people are ready. The time is now. The choice is yours.

With urgency, conviction, unshakable hope, and deep respect, I am
— *Mary Knapp*

Chapter 12

The Power of We, Building the Movement for Truth and Healing

History has taught us a hard truth: governments do not give up power willingly. Transparency is not gifted—it is demanded. Justice is not handed down from on high—it is wrestled from the grip of those who profit from lies and corruption. Healing does not arrive passively—it is built, brick by brick, by people who refuse to be silenced, divided, or diminished.

If we are waiting for someone else to save us, we will wait until the end of time. But if **we the people** rise together—citizens, whistleblowers, researchers, healers, journalists, faith leaders, activists, business owners, survivors, and truth-tellers—we can forge the only path strong enough to pierce through decades of deceit: a Truth and Reconciliation Commission, born of the people's demand and sustained by the people's participation.

Step 1: Anchor the Why
Every movement begins with a shared truth. The why is simple and undeniable:
- Lies and corruption have poisoned our institutions.
- Trust has collapsed.
- Families and communities are fractured.
- People are suffering—mentally, emotionally, economically, spiritually.

A Truth and Reconciliation Commission is not an option—it is a survival mechanism. It is how we prevent history from repeating itself, how we restore dignity, and how we reclaim sovereignty.

Action: Create a simple, unifying declaration—a *People's Mandate for Truth*—that can be shared, signed, and amplified as the backbone of the movement.

Step 2: Mobilize the Multi-Track Front

A TRC will only come into being when all tracks push together—government, citizens, whistleblowers, healers, researchers, business, media, and more. Each has its lane, but together they form a system.

Government Track
- Push lawmakers, governors, and mayors to issue resolutions of support.
- Lobby for executive orders to establish commissions at local and state levels while pressing nationally.
- Demand hearings on corruption, censorship, and rights violations.

Citizen Track
- Build grassroots hubs in towns, cities, and states.
- Launch petitions, local truth circles, and community forums.
- Use alternative platforms to bypass censorship and reach the people directly.

Whistleblower & Research Track
- Protect whistleblowers with legal defense funds and safe networks.
- Partner with independent researchers to compile and verify evidence.
- Create an open-source archive of documents, testimonies, and data.

Healing Track
- Organize trauma-informed spaces for citizens to process grief and rage.
- Mobilize faith leaders, therapists, and healers to guide collective recovery.
- Pair justice with healing: truth-telling must restore, not retraumatize.

Business & Funding Track
- Engage ethical business leaders to fund infrastructure.
- Frame corruption as an economic parasite that destroys honest markets.
- Organize boycotts of corporations complicit in censorship, surveillance, or exploitation.

Journalism & Storytelling Track
- Build alliances with independent journalists, podcasters, filmmakers, and authors.
- Collect and share survivor stories, putting a human face on systemic crimes.
- Break propaganda walls by amplifying truth in compelling, viral ways.

Public Opinion Track
- Shape a moral wave of outrage and hope that makes silence impossible.
- Coordinate marches, vigils, and symbolic "Truth Days of Remembrance."
- Frame TRCs as patriotic, moral, and inevitable.

Step 3: Create a Coordinated Strategy
- **National Truth Network:** Link local movements into a national body.
- **Cross-Track Councils:** Representatives from each track meet regularly to align strategy.
- **Digital Hub:** Build an online platform to track progress, host resources, and connect citizens.

Step 4: Apply Pressure at Every Point
- **Legislative Pressure:** Flood lawmakers with calls, petitions, and citizen resolutions.
- **Media Pressure:** Expose censorship, highlight victims, and shame perpetrators.
- **Economic Pressure:** Target complicit corporations and institutions financially.
- **Cultural Pressure:** Use art, film, music, and ritual to make the TRC a cultural demand—not just a political one.

Step 5: Safeguard the Movement

- **Security:** Protect whistleblowers, organizers, and survivors from intimidation.
- **Integrity:** Adopt strict ethical codes to prevent infiltration or corruption.
- **Unity:** Refuse to be divided by partisan traps. This is bigger than left or right—it's about humanity.

Step 6: Build Toward the Commission

Every petition signed, every story told, every hearing demanded is a stepping stone. Movements do not succeed overnight, but through relentless persistence.

The goal is to make a Truth and Reconciliation Commission so urgent, so obvious, and so morally undeniable that leaders cannot ignore it without exposing themselves as complicit.

This is how we win: not by waiting for permission, but by unleashing the **Power of We**—millions of voices aligned in one demand: **Truth. Justice. Healing.**

Chapter 13

Healing and Transformation

The work of a Truth and Reconciliation Commission is not merely procedural. It is not just about gathering testimony, reviewing documents, or exposing the machinery of deception. At its deepest level, a TRC is about the restoration of humanity itself.

Human beings cannot thrive under lies. Our bodies, minds, and souls revolt against corruption, manipulation, and the unrelenting dissonance of knowing that what we are told is not what is true. **Truth is a primary nutrient for the human spirit—just as essential as clean air, pure water, and nourishing food.** Justice is the structure that allows truth to matter, to take root, and to endure. Healing is the fruit that grows when truth and justice are honored. Together, these are not optional—they are the very conditions of human survival and flourishing.

This is why a Truth and Reconciliation Commission is not simply desirable—it is indispensable. It is the only framework capable of holding the scale of harm, acknowledging the wounds inflicted, and guiding us toward repair. Without it, we risk calcifying into bitterness, despair, and endless cycles of retaliation. With it, we stand a chance at wholeness.

The Need for Collective Grief Work

A nation that has endured generational betrayal and trauma must first allow itself to grieve. We must name the losses: trust broken, families divided, livelihoods destroyed, communities fractured, sovereignty stolen, hope dimmed. Without a space for collective mourning, we remain frozen—unable to move forward.

Grief is not weakness. Grief is the pathway to renewal.

A TRC provides the ceremonial and civic container for grief. Testimonies become more than personal accounts—they become rituals of mourning, woven into a shared story of loss and resilience. This collective grief work dissolves isolation and allows a people to finally say: *We see. We feel. We remember. And we will not carry this in silence anymore.*

Restorative Practices as Pathways to Renewal

Punishment alone cannot heal what has been broken. Retribution without restoration leaves only hollow victories. What we require are practices that acknowledge harm, repair relationships where possible, and reweave the torn fabric of community.

Restorative circles, mediated dialogues, truth-telling ceremonies, and reconciliation gatherings must become part of our civic life. These are not luxuries—they are survival strategies for a fractured nation. A TRC can normalize these practices, embedding them into schools, communities, workplaces, and even government processes—creating a cultural shift toward repair rather than endless harm.

AI-Assisted Healing Tools

For the first time in history, we have technologies that can extend and deepen our healing. Artificial Intelligence, when harnessed ethically, can assist in ways human capacity alone cannot. Imagine:

- **AI-guided truth journaling** to help individuals process trauma in structured ways.
- **Justice visualization therapies** that allow victims to symbolically see wrongs acknowledged and repaired.
- **Biofeedback mapping** that reveals stress patterns in real time and offers personalized practices for release.
- **Restorative justice simulations** where victims and offenders can prepare for mediated encounters in safe, AI-assisted environments.

Far from replacing human connection, AI can serve as a supportive companion—scaling healing practices across millions of lives, while preserving the core human needs for empathy and presence.

Reclaiming Sovereignty

Healing cannot be complete without sovereignty. Sovereignty means reclaiming authority over our bodies, our communities, and our nation. Lies and corruption are forms of theft—they steal autonomy and erode the very foundation of freedom.

A TRC is the mechanism by which sovereignty can be reclaimed. By exposing what was hidden, acknowledging abuse of power, and creating systemic safeguards, sovereignty ceases to be abstract and becomes lived reality.

Rewriting the Social Contract

The social contract—the unspoken agreement between people and their institutions—has been shattered. Trust has been violated so deeply that repair requires not just reform, but reimagining.

Through the work of a TRC, we have the opportunity to rewrite the social contract:

- One that insists on transparency as the default, not secrecy.
- One that centers human dignity, not exploitation.
- One that weaves truth, justice, and healing into governance itself.
- One that prepares future generations not to blindly trust authority, but to participate with vigilance and shared responsibility.

Transformation

Healing is not the end of the story—it is the beginning of transformation. From the ashes of betrayal can emerge a society more honest, more humane, and more resilient than the one that was lost. A TRC offers us not only the chance to heal from the past, but to shape a future where truth is honored, justice is real, and healing is ongoing.

The transformation we seek is nothing less than the rebirth of sovereignty, the reclamation of humanity, and the renewal of trust in one another. A Truth and Reconciliation Commission is the vessel that can carry us there.

An Invitation to You

This work cannot be outsourced. Healing is not something a commission, a president, or a government can hand down to us. It begins with us—citizens, families, neighbors, truth-tellers, healers, seekers. A Truth and Reconciliation Commission can provide the structure, but it is our willingness to engage that gives it life.

So I ask you:
- Where in your own story is there grief that longs to be voiced?
- Where have you witnessed harm that must be named?
- Where can you contribute your gifts—whether as a citizen, a professional, a whistleblower, a researcher, or a neighbor—to the collective work of truth and repair?

The transformation of a nation begins with the transformation of its people. Each act of honesty, each conversation rooted in dignity, each moment of courage adds to the momentum of healing.

You are needed. Your voice matters. Your presence matters. Your willingness to grieve, to demand truth, to insist on justice, and to participate in healing is how we reclaim sovereignty and rewrite the social contract.

The Commission may be the vessel, but **you are the lifeblood.**

Let us move forward together—not only to expose what has been done to us, but to create what we will become.

Chapter 14

The Future We Choose

History stands at a crossroads. One road drags us deeper into the machinery of control: algorithms deciding our freedoms, technocrats rewriting what it means to be human, global powers harvesting our data, our bodies, even our souls. That road ends in a sterile world where sovereignty is surrendered, relationships are replaced by simulations, and truth itself becomes programmable.

But there is another road. It is harder. Braver. The road that demands we remember what it means to be human—and refuse to surrender it.

Humanity is not a flaw to be corrected, nor an error in code to be rewritten. We are flesh and spirit, reason and mystery, community and individuality. We are born with an intrinsic need for truth, fairness, and love. To deny this is to deny life itself.

A Rallying Call to Action

The future we want will not arrive on its own. It must be fought for, demanded, and built with our hands, our voices, and our unbreakable will.

Without truth, there is no trust. Without justice, there is no peace. Without healing, there is no future.

The time for passivity is over. The time for silence is over. Each of us has a role: citizens demanding transparency, healers tending to wounds, journalists exposing the shadows, whistleblowers breaking the chains of secrecy, activists refusing to yield, faith leaders calling us higher, and communities writing new covenants for sovereignty and freedom.

We are not waiting for permission. We are not waiting for saviors. We are the ones we have been waiting for.

The future we choose will either enslave us—or set us free. And the choice is not in the hands of the few. It rests with all of us, here and now.

Rise. Demand truth. Build justice. Choose healing. Protect humanity.
The future is watching.

Epilogue

A Benediction for Truth

May truth, long buried, rise into the light.
May justice, long delayed, flow at last like a river.
May healing, long deferred, reach every heart, every home, every nation.

May we remember that to be human is to seek fairness, to honor dignity, to belong to one another.
May we reclaim what was stolen—our voices, our communities, our trust—and weave them back into wholeness.

May the grief of generations be honored, not silenced.
May the courage of those who spoke, who suffered, who stood, never be forgotten.
May reconciliation continue until every wound is seen, every story heard, every soul restored.

And may we, in this time of reckoning, step forward not with vengeance, but with vision;
not with fear, but with faith;
not with despair, but with the quiet, unshakable knowing:

That truth heals.
That justice redeems.
That love endures.

Go forward, then, into the future we choose—together.

www.ingramcontent.com/pod-product-compliance
Lightning Source LLC
Chambersburg PA
CBHW032154020426

42334CB00016B/1278